What Do You Mean Your Dog Ate Your Timecard?

A Look at the Blue-Collar Worker

Written by R.A. Challis
Illustrations by Rose Ann Coon

PublishAmerica
Baltimore

First printing

ISBN: 1-60836-499-2
PUBLISHED BY PUBLISHAMERICA, LLLP
www.publishamerica.com
Baltimore

Printed in the United States of America

Introduction

This book is a view of the everyday worker and how he or she sees “live, government and the world as a whole”. Many times corporate management see the worker in a different light then the worker sees him or herself. The way the term Blue Collar worker has gone from a stigma to a badge of pride, and why the way America looks at the Blue collar workers should be viewed differently

Before I start I wish to express a little story that I think shows how we should view worker growth.

Two men are walking in the woods as they walk along they run across a very large bear the bear starts chasing them with the attempt to eat them. As the men run along the narrow path one stops and sets down and takes a part of running shoes out of his bag. He starts to put them on when the other man says “Hey! What are you doing?” Those won’t help you out run the bear he says. The first man said “no but I will out run you!”

The man who thinks outside the box, looking ahead of others will always stay ahead of any competition. I dedicate this book to all managements that I have reported to or worked with as an hourly worker and a salaried manager.

Chapter One

For many years now there has been a major change in the work effect of the blue-collar worker. The ongoing pride in ones job no longer excited to the extent that was found in the work place say 20 years ago. Many times you hear how one cannot committed to the basic requirements of the job he or she is required to do, let alone going above or beyond just for the sake of self pride.

This at times no longer excited in most workers I think because of not being instilled with good work effects at a young age. Most are told by not only their peers but also the media that they are owned something by the system from the get go but don't know what this is. Many times they wonder from job to job seeking this but not knowing what or where they should be looking for it or what it is. Do you ever stop and ask yourself why you get up and go to work every day? Or do you just do it because, "well, I have to."

Think for a moment about why many times you will find that it's self accomplishment that drives you, the need to do better than the father or mother that raised you or at the least gain their approval but to no avail. This approval rarely happens and then not fully so we wonder through life thinking that we have a poor job a poor life. But in fact it's pretty darn good we're free, we can change jobs any time we like, and we arc only limited by our own drive and ambitions.

The average worker does not wish to grow or to push to achieve a higher level of prosperity in his or her life if it means they have to work harder or longer hours to achieve this goal. They wish only to gain more time to play and or maybe not do anything but waste time, this desire to do nothing stems I believe from the generation who strive for the need to be self involved only with ones person only forsaking any other person's feelings and or needs. Never really committing to anything or anyone and for damn sure not a job. I call it a job because no one what's to make a long-term career they're looking for that fast track to fame and fortune as presented on TV or the movies. Which of course rarely comes to anyone? The only reel way to build a future takes hard work and long-term commitment.

Chapter Two

OK, let's break it down to the basics. Let's start with oneself; are you happy to get there? You can't do this by being someone else, so who are you? Why are you here? And do you have goals? Are you a carbon copy of someone else? We all get our personality by years of watching and

developing from others, what we wish to be like. For example I had my dad Bill Challis, actor John Wayne and a special man, my father-in-law Jack Boggs who taught me how to be a man.

- Treat others as you would wish to be treated.
- Never start a fight but never back down when you know you are right. but at the same time pick your battles in order to win the war,
- Never hit a woman no matter what no matter why, treat her like a lady because you would only be with a lady to disrespect her is to disrespect yourself.
- Remember a job worth doing is worth doing right the first time.
- And always give a man a fair days worth of work for a fair days pay. If he ask for 8 hours give him/her 8 ½ hours.

You know one of today's problems is that we live in a throwaway society; this goes from cars to TV's to marriages.

Most people do not take their wedding vows very sacredly; it doesn't say I take you till I get tired of you. It say till death do we part for better or worse for richer and for poorer, in sickness and in good health. I think divorces have become too easy to get and should be thought out more; it maybe lies with the fact that most people want that easy fast fix and don't wish to work at it, marriage is like a job you have to work hard and be committed to getting better in order to gain the fruits of your labor.

If you try to please everyone else, but not the ones near you, you will surely fail. It is important to insure that the ones near you are happy and has all their needs meet. If you think you need to meet your needs before your love ones you become very selfish and lacking in many of the true traits that are the mark of a real man. And you show a large amount of lack of responsibility.

Chapter Three

OK let break down some of the problems starting with the media. Many times the media talks about how the public feels about a subject, but the problem with this is the media usually knows little of what the true American worker feels or needs. They don't know because they have

lost touch with the common man. He's not in Hollywood that's for sure or playing pro sports for a living.

The average worker goes to work making a below survival wage trying to take care of a family. Many times it takes both husband and wife working in order to survive. With both the wife and husband working they have little time for politics, let alone forgoing public affairs which slip to the wayside mainly because no one can see much past their next paycheck. But what they do care about and see very little of is the government working on the common workers needs such as how to stop price gouging at the gas pump, or how to stop illegal immigrants taking their jobs here in America or jobs going overseas or to Mexico, and the need for some type of government reduction.

We spent too much time taking care of all the other nations and not resolving the problems here at home, this shows a large majority of people that the government really does not care about it own citizens. With all that said, the government needs to think about how it can help the children right here in this nation and save our own future. Not spending tax payer's moneys' to support programs to help other nations when we have not resolved problems here.

Many times the government rewards parents for being single parents and not trying to raise their children as a family unit. A child raised without a father leads to a low self-esteem and a poor understanding of proper values in life. Many experts will agree with the fact that both parents play important parts in raising a child. The mother cannot provide everything a child needs. I don't care how you wish to look at it, nor can a father raising a child provide the full gamete of needs that a woman provides. The over-whelming amount of children reared without both parents' present shows up in society today in many forms and ways, one of the most common is the "you owe me" attitude.

Crime and violence is at an all-time high. TV, the internet, and movies are corrupt with massive problems and with no responsibility for their actions; for example: female singer performing provocatively and then complaining about how bad this country is. I say don't be part of the problem and then complain about it, try setting an example.

It's really not that hard practice what you preach; don't ask your children to do something you're not willing to do yourself. Earlier I said you lead through example this applies to both work and home; the same rules both at home and work and private life must prevail. This belief doesn't come from religious beliefs and the person who claims it does may not understand just basic morality. How hard is that you know what's right by how you feel inside, don't do it if it feels wrong, and think before you do? For those of us who belief in a higher power and conscious it just cements our point of view.

The big car companies are now lying off workers because they can't sell cars; well maybe they need to remember if you send jobs oversea then there went the car buyers. Also maybe it's not the workers fault that the car is not up to par with a foreign made but how the upper management, the manner in which it is built (what happen to making a good product no matter how much it cost you and selling it for a far price) this can't be done by selling a car as though it's a house; with extremely high interest rates and extended payment terms reveals it.

When the big auto manufactures ask for a federal government bailout they usually repay their notes in a timely manner, thus it's not a complete loss to the tax payers, compared to when the stock exchange asks for a bailout.

You talk about wages being too high, fine start at the top, boy that hit home did it not! Unfortunately, big business cut the little guys wages or eliminates their position. Lord forbid that the blue collar worker actually make a profit from his hard work! In reality, we ought to sell products at a price the common man can afford then he will not need more wages, but someone has to start the process. Who's going to give in, the worker or the upper management? Soon there will not be anything to give in to if we keep going like this.

Chapter Four

OK! Now here my view on the elderly, in years past the younger generation took care of the older when they reached that age, many of us live in homes that in the past would have had three generations living there, now this is not the way; it's almost a negative stigma that prevents multigenerational housing. This is why we have a larger amount of older citizens needing the government support to survive. How sad is that? Stop thinking of just yourself and think of your family as a whole; that means all older and younger members of your family count. Treat them as they should be treated.

Chapter Five

Many managers may believe in one method or another, but use that of their bosses or of the organization. Their upbringing and personal, pre-management experiences tell them that a certain method is correct. Some mangers were educated, formally or informally, in a certain method. Others have had no training and have had to employ their own methods. Theirs may resemble one of the established systems. Also, sometimes the workers force, or allow, a manager to adopt a particular method of management style.

The people in a department may cause a manager to use particular tactics. For example, if a department is cohesive, supportive, and responsive, a manager will be able to apply many of the behavioral methods. Behavioral methods rely on good relations between manager and worker. They also require the participation of the workers. Conversely, if the workers refuse to participate, the behavioral methods will fail, which may force a manager to employ classical methods. But if all possible he should try to adopt a method that will allow equal respect.

Behavioral methods generally depend on workers taking responsibility for their work and on workers earning their managers' trust and vice-versa. Responsibility for completing the work means completing it at a high level of quality and efficiency without a large amount of supervision. Some people cannot, or will not, make this commitment. They may try to take advantage of the system and do much less than their share. They should not be surprised, then, when the manager employs some of the more severe methods such as reprimands.

Also, the manager must trust the worker to work independently. Trust takes time to earn; the worker must first demonstrate that he or she can be depended on before autonomy is granted. Workers who do not take the time and do not make the effort to earn a their managers' trust should not be surprised if they are treated differently from those who have proven themselves although a manager should treat all the same, it may not be always possible. Individual differences may also exist. A manager may use behavioral methods on all but one person in a department if that person fails to respond to those methods.

Chapter Six

The classical method is a strict bipartisan method of where management is in a superior position to the manual laborer; they the employees are referred to as "pee-on/ plebeians" not worthy of equality or respect based upon their socio-economic status, spearheaded upon how much or how little the employee is educated and skilled.

Finally, one of the difficult jobs for any manager is trying to find motivational techniques that will work. Here are some tools I have been trained on in the past. Recognizing achievement, work itself as a motivation, giving the team member responsibility, and allowing growth.

The people in a department may cause a manager to use particular tactics. For example, if a department is cohesive, supportive, and responsive, a manager will be able to apply many of the behavioral methods. Behavioral methods rely on good relations between manager and worker. They also require the participation of the workers. Conversely, if the workers refuse to participate, the behavioral methods will fail, which may force a manager to employ classical methods. But if all possible he should try to adopt a method that will allow equal respect.

Individual differences may also exist. A manager may use behavioral methods on all but one person in a department if that person fails to respond to those methods. Behavioral methods generally depend on workers taking responsibility for their work and on workers earning their managers' trust and vice-versa.

Responsibility for completing the work means completing it at a high level of quality and efficiency without a large amount of supervision. Some people cannot, or will not, make this commitment. They may try to take advantage of the system and do much less than their share. They should not be surprised, then, when the manager employs some of the more severe methods such as reprimands. Also, the manager must trust the worker to work independently. Trust takes time to earn; the worker must first demonstrate that he or she can be depended on before autonomy is granted. Workers who do not take the time and do not make the effort to earn a their managers' trust should not be surprised if they are treated differently from those who have proven themselves although a manager should treat all the same, it may not be always possible.

Chapter Seven

Motivating the Worker

Finally, one of the difficult jobs for any manager is trying to find motivational techniques that will work. Here are some things IE: tools I have been trained on in the past. Recognizing achievement, work itself is a motivation, giving the team member Responsibility, and allowing growth. Many changes taking place in the workplace are likely to increase employee employees' level of stress, insecurity, and frustration.

Some organizations are pursuing short-term financial gains at a high cost. Organizations that focus on providing humane, supportive, and empowering work environments for their employees will have a strong competitive advantage in the modern workplace.

Organizational culture consists of the values, symbols, stories, heroes, and rites that have special meaning for a company's employees.

Culture represents the intangible part of an

organization. Many firms are now attempting to develop organizational cultures that are helpful in motivating their employees and keeping them committed to the company. Recent study of recent mergers found that incompatible cultures were the primary cause of failures. An organization's culture is something that is impossible to duplicate. The functions of an organizational culture include:

Encouragement of cooperation

Not all ideas are earth-shattering, but they need to be voiced. Having a creative individual with vision of what the company could be is invaluable to say the least. He/She looks outside the box—don't beat them down with negative criticism or "can't be done" philosophy. Generating ideas is what keeps the doors open in business. The goal is to take what the CEO/Owner started and run with it, making it the biggest and best company in its field. Even small businesses or home based businesses need vision.

Chapter Eight

Greater Efficiency in Decision Making

Competence and good organization needs to be a top down to bottom up communication style. Too often upper management fail to listen what the mid-management is telling them. Allot of it is pride or feeling of superiority over the little guy. But the little guy doing the work is what is keeping the doors open. Entry-level management i.e.; working supervisors and leadsman/women know the temperature of the blue collar workers motivational aspect.

They understand the frustrations and satisfactions of their team members and can relate them to mid-management more efficiently because they are in the trenches working side-by side the blue collar worker. In fact the blue collar worker might have ideas that save the company thousands of dollars once implemented.

Providing a subtle organizational control system.

By using the internal; grapevine you can release official and unofficial information that would allow redirection in many cases and steer off problems. One must be careful of how and what is released because it will take a short time for this datum to travel through a company. It is a good practice to use only unofficial information that you wish to release and use corporate channels for other information to be released. This is often referred to by production departments as a little "Payton's Place."

Reducing the need for some types of communication and facilitating the interpretation of communication. The corporate formal means of communication carriers a stigma of limited trust by the common blue collar worker because of past broken promises and half-truths. If a company be that the level of supervisor, manager or above makes a promise to a blue collar worker they must try to fulfill that agreement at all costs. This lack of trust that has been generated from company failures to fulfill verbal agreements perpetuates the mental desire that a union has something to offer. And builds an us against them attitude.

Emotional attachment and commitment to the organization. If a blue collar feels that the company is loyal and faithful to them they will begin to develop a sense of loyalty to the company, this together will build a stronger bond of work ethics and a desire to see the company succeed.

Providing shared interpretations of experiences perception. If an employee feels that they have buy-in and that the company, or supervisor, or manager respect their previous experiences and knowledge and is more likely to collaborate in the problem solving process and could add valued information to resolve issues and problems. (i.e.: Steering Committees, Kaizen, Trouble-shooting committees).

Providing justification of employee behavior.

The elements of an organizational culture include:

Values (i.e., deep-seated, personal standards that influence our moral judgments)

- Do I leave 20 minutes earlier than the drive time so that I won't be late to work? Do I arrive just in the nick-of-time, feeling harried or lass' fare about clocking in with the "I'm here aren't I" attitude?
- Do I have a sexual encounter with my boss so that I will get promoted or recognized on future projects that will help my career? (Hint: It doesn't work that way in the long run!)
- Do I devote 100% of my ability while on the job or do I just look busy when the bosses are in the area?
- Am I a gossip carrier? Gossip is poising the well at work; it diminishes harmony and good will towards employees. It is usually based on one incident taken out of context and extrapolated and conjured to be really damaging to another persons credibility or ability to do their job.

Symbols (i.e., things that stand for or suggest something else). Show a toddler the golden arches of McDonalds™ and they can tell you that's where they want to go eat and play at. The value of excellent marketing techniques is essential to business growth. Bush Beans™ uses a dog named Duke to tell a story about the company in a humorous setting.

Another way to identify ones team members is to divide the workers into social groups. Metal Containers Company has Red/Gold and Blue/Silver for the 24/7 / 364 days of operation. The colors represent 12 hour shifts for a 24 hours period; they have two half-hour overlapping of time for communication briefings. The company builds group dynamics by have many social events with the employees and their families and develops team players among its members. To keep moral high there is competition between the Red/Gold and Blue/Silver teams to get the production numbers higher than the other team. There is allotting of pressure placed on the individual worker to do their part as a team member.

They also implement activities that engage the spouse of the employee to develop a family atmosphere within the global company.

Narratives (i.e., written or spoken accounts such as stories, legends or myths used by members of an organization to make sense of their experiences and to express their feelings and beliefs)

HMS Realty uses little stories, sarcasms, and antidotes' to tell people they are stupid to be renting when they can own a nice home.

Mary Kay Cosmetics tells her beauty consultants her story of struggles as a single woman trying to make it in 'a man's world' and now has a multi-million dollar industry. Her message is she made it going door-to-door and so can you.

Heroes (i.e., company role models)

Everyone knows this person he/she looks professional in company attire, is usually charismatic and can get the

job done. They usually have a Type a personality; self driven and motivated, intelligent, creative/innovative, volunteers' to be a leader, can be a pain in the butt at times. They are an embodiment of staying busy all the time, usually a multi-tasking specialist. They appear to thrive on deadlines and getting the job done when others may say its impossible; they seem to pull the rabbit out of the hat and save the day.

Rites (i.e., combine cultural forms into public performance).

We all have heard of "Rites of passages" of which we see a mental torch being handed down to our successor. It could be a banquet for giving out plaques or certificates acknowledging ones work as being superior to another's. It is the "Atta-boys!" of recognition, sometimes in the form of bonus money or free tickets to some popular event.

Rituals (i.e., relatively simple combinations of repetitive behaviors). To foster a creative and productive environment where employees are motivated to achieve exceptional performance, the organization's culture needs to empower its employees. Many organizations create feelings of learned helplessness among employees. Empowerment seeks to break the spiral of powerlessness by giving employees a sense of real control.

Chapter Nine

The five stages of the empowerment process are:

Stage 1—Conditions leading to a psychological state of powerlessness (e.g., supervision, reward systems).

Stage 2—The use of managerial strategies and techniques (e.g., goal setting, feedback systems, modeling).

Stage 3—To provide self-efficacy information to subordinates using four sources (e.g., enactive attainment, vicarious experience, verbal persuasion, emotional arousal and removal of stage 1 conditions).

Stage 4—Results in empowering experience of subordinates.

Step 5—Leading to behavioral effects (e.g., initiation/ persistence of behavior to accomplish task objectives)

Chapter Ten

Organizational Culture

Develop and maintain an organizational culture that reinforces the core values of the firm. Align the culture of

an organization with its mission and strategic objectives. Use a variety of methods (e.g., stories, rites and ceremonies, and symbols) to communicate organizational culture to employees.

Allow subcultures and even countercultures to coexist with the dominant culture when they support the strategic objectives of the firm. Assess the current culture of a firm as the first step in developing a plan for changing it. Identify the underlying causes of resistance to changing corporate culture as a basis for developing a plan for ultimately transforming it. Recognize that cultural change in organizations will take time. Ensure that employees possess the job-specific knowledge, skills, and abilities as well as the maturity to benefit from an empowerment program. Remember that sharing power with employees (i.e., empowerment) actually enhances the power of a manager in many cases as opposed to diminishing it. Establish what "ethical behavior" means for your firm and communicate these standards to employees using a variety of mechanisms (e.g., employee handbooks, mission statements, annual reports, memos). Develop a "system" and a culture that emphasize the importance of ethical behavior in the workplace. Use managerial policies and practices to reward ethical behavior and to punish unethical behavior. Develop and maintain an organizational culture that reinforces the core values of the firm. Align the culture of an organization with its mission and strategic objectives. Use a variety of methods (e.g., stories, rites and ceremonies, and symbols) to communicate organizational culture to employees. Allow subcultures and even countercultures to coexist with the dominant culture when they support the strategic objectives of the firm. Assess the current culture of a firm as the first step in developing a plan for changing it. Identify the underlying causes of resistance to changing corporate culture as a basis for developing a plan for ultimately transforming it. Recognize that cultural change in organizations will take time. Ensure that employees possess the job-specific knowledge, skills, and abilities as well as the maturity to benefit from an empowerment program. Remember that sharing power with employees (i.e., empowerment) actually enhances the power of a manager in many cases as opposed to diminishing it. Establish what “ethical behavior” means for your firm and communicate these standards to employees using a variety of mechanisms (e.g., employee handbooks, mission statements, annual reports, memos). Develop a “system” and a culture that emphasize the importance of ethical behavior in the workplace. Use managerial policies and practices to reward ethical behavior and to punish unethical behavior.

Chapter Eleven

Blue-collar is a term for what some refer to as the working class. A blue-collar worker is differentiated from white-collar and service employees, in that the blue-collar worker earns an hourly wage (as opposed to the white-collar salary) and performs manual labor (as opposed to

the service-industry worker). Blue collar work may be skilled or unskilled, and may involve factory work, building and construction trades, law enforcement, mechanical work, maintenance or technical installations. The white-collar worker, by contrast, performs non-manual labor often in an office; and the service industry worker performs non-manual labor involving customer interaction, entertainment, retail sales, and the like.

This term occasionally carries a stereotype based on historical perspective, but is rarely perceived to be a negative one. The blue-collar worker in the United States is an embodiment of the American mythos of a work ethic and the dignity of labor. Rightly or wrongly, some blue-collar jobs, such as those of janitors and unskilled laborers, may carry negative stereotypes from perceptions that they represent minimal ability. Most, however, involve levels of specialized skill that carry no stigma, and are on the contrary a source of pride.

The term derives from the dress codes of workplaces. Industrial and manual workers wear durable clothing that can be soiled or scrapped at work. A popular element of such "work clothes" has been, and still is, a light or navy blue shirt. Blue is also a popular color for coveralls.

The popularity of the color blue among persons who do manual labor is contrasted to the ubiquitous white dress shirt that, historically, has been standard attire in office environments. This obvious color-coding has been used to identify a difference in socio-economic class. This distinction is growing more blurred, however, with the increasing importance of skilled labor, and the growth of non-laboring, but low-paying, service sector jobs.

Blue-collar can also be used as an adjective to describe the environment of the blue-collar worker: e.g. a blue-collar neighborhood, job, restaurant, bar, etc., or a situation describing the use of manual effort and the strength required to do so.

Some distinctive elements of blue-collar work are the lesser requirements for formal academic education which is needed to succeed in other types of work. Blue-collar work typically is wage-labor and entails a labor model that involves a 1-minute-accurate clock-in system. Usually, the pay for such occupation is lower than that of the white-collar worker, although higher than many entry-level service occupations. Sometimes the work conditions can be strenuous or hazardous. Skilled blue-collar work often pays as well or better than careers requiring professional post-graduate degrees.

Blue collar workers exist in varying proportions throughout the industrial world, though several locations, such as the United States state of Pennsylvania, particularly the cities of Allentown and Pittsburgh, contain large numbers of blue-collar workers and both cities have sometimes been highlighted in popular culture because of their blue-collar reputations.

With the movement of many Western nations towards service based economy, the Blue-collar workforce has steadily decreased in size. At the same time skilled Blue-collar workers, mainly trade's people working in the building industry have seen rapidly rising wages. Blue-collar worker supervisors direct, help, and train workers in physically active jobs.

Chapter Twelve

Have you ever wondered why some jobs are called "blue-collar" while others are called "white collar?" The names are from the color of uniforms or shirts workers wear. People who work in construction trades or manufacturing often wear uniforms. In the past, they were often darker blue and made of durable material. (For many jobs, this is still the case). Hence, the term "blue collar." People who worked behind desks usually wore white shirts with ties.

Nowadays, blue-collar is a term given to jobs that require a lot of physical activity. Construction and manufacturing are two examples of industries where workers have a high level of physical activity. Regardless of the type of work being done, supervisors have many of the same tasks.

Supervisors have many duties that involve personnel management. For example, they hire, fire, and evaluate employees. They also resolve worker problems or assist workers in solving problems. In addition, supervisors train new employees.

When starting new projects, supervisors estimate the number of workers and the amount of materials needed to complete the project. They may create a budget that shows this information. Before beginning the project, supervisors analyze its requirements. Then they plan and establish work goals. These goals may involve coordinating work with other departments. Supervisors then assign tasks to workers. They keep records of how work is progressing. If work falls behind schedule, they revise tasks or reassign workers to improve progress.

In manufacturing plants, supervisors make sure the machinery is set up and operating properly. They adjust machinery controls, test machines, and repair or order the repair of broken machinery. They also create work schedules, oversee workers, and make sure the work is done correctly and on time.

In construction companies, supervisors lay out construction sites and assign workers to specific jobs. They also order supplies and equipment. In addition, supervisors discuss prices and work details with customers. They interpret design plans for other workers as well as inspect their work. Supervisors often work alongside the worker

Chapter Thirteen

Self Motivations

To be a successful manager/motivator you must first understand that you cannot motivate anyone. You can only create an environment that encourages and promotes the employee's self motivation. Someone once said that motivation is getting people to do what you want them to do because **they want** to do it. The challenge is to give them a reason to want to do it; doing it will satisfy a need they have. You have to tune in to their need, not yours.

Secondly, you must also know what kind of behavior you want the employee to demonstrate. In other words, what do you want the employee to do differently?

For example, do you want the employee to come to work on time? Greet the customers in a friendly manner? Complete forms correctly? Assume more responsibility? You must be clear about your expectations before you can communicate them to your employees.

The third important thing to keep in mind is that you are the critical component in the motivation process. Your actions set the tone. Many managers embrace the “carrot-on-the-stick” approach to motivating employees. These practices take the form of incentive programs, promises of rewards and bonuses. Others employ the symbolic “whip” or “club” by emphasizing the negative results of their behavior.

For example, a manager might say, “If you don’t start getting to work on time, you’ll be fired” or “You’ll never get ahead if you continue to make these kinds of mistakes.” The problem is that these short-term “quick fixes” create no permanent behavior change.

Do you really encourage people and bring out the best in them, or do you manage them through intimidation and threats? What motivation methods have you tried? Did they work? If so, for how long? Sometimes the simplest things can motivate a person to perform better a how’s your day, how’s your family, or just saying hello every day. if you allow a person to feel they have buy in to some form of their job they will feel more like they have ownership in the task at hand and will perform better just out of pride. It is not uncommon for a team member to feel left out just based on their perception and not what is really going on so it becomes vary important to insure they always feel part of the team.

A **blue-collar worker** is an idiom referring to a member of the working class who performs manual labor and earns an hourly wage. Blue-collar workers are distinguished from Tertiary sector of industry *service* workers and from *white-collar* workers, whose jobs are not considered manual labor. However, some service workers are also often referred to as blue-collar workers. Traditionally, white-collar workers earn a monthly or annual salary rather than an hourly wage, although paying white-collar workers by the hour is an increasing practice, especially among independent tech contractors. Blue-collar work may be skilled or unskilled, and may involve factory work, construction building and construction trades, law enforcement, mechanical work,

Maintenance, repair and operations maintenance or technical installations. The white-collar worker, by contrast, performs non-manual labor often in an office; and the service industry worker performs labor involving customer interaction, entertainment, retail and outside sales, and the like. Some service industry workers differ as they perform tasks that are mostly unskilled in the service sector.

The term blue-collar occasionally carries a stereotype based on historical perspective. The blue-collar worker in the United States is an embodiment of the American mythos of a work ethic and the dignity of labor. Blue-collar workers take pride in their jobs. Some blue-collar jobs, such as those of janitors and assembly line workers, may carry negative stereotypes from perceptions that they represent minimal ability, or that the people in those positions were too lazy to obtain a better job or were poorly educated. Most involve levels of specialized skill that carry no stigma, and are contrarily a source of pride.

Industrial and manual workers wear durable clothing that can be soiled or scrapped at work. A popular element of such "work clothes" has been, and still is, a light or navy blue shirt. Blue is also a popular color for coveralls, and will usually carry a name tag of the company/ establishment on one side, and the individual's name on the other. Often these items are bought by the company and laundered by the establishment as well.

The popularity of the color blue among persons who do

manual labor is contrasted to the ubiquitous white dress shirt that, historically, has been standard attire in office environments. This obvious color-coding has been used to identify a difference in socio-economic class. This distinction is growing more blurred, however, with the increasing importance of skilled labor, and the growth of non-laboring, but low-paying, service sector jobs. Blue-collar can also be used as an adjective to describe the environment of the blue-collar worker: e.g. a blue-collar neighborhood, job, restaurant, bar, etc., or a situation describing the use of manual effort and the strength required to do so.

Some misnomers of blue-collar workers are the lesser requirements for formal academic education which is needed to succeed in other types of Jobs, with many blue-collar jobs requiring only a High School Diploma or GED use to be the normal requirements. Many times in today's increasingly automated factories it is required to have an increased education. Many industrial Mantainece Mechanics are required to have a high level of skill and education to work on highly computerized equipment. The need for such workers is very much on the increase throughout the world. Blue-collar work typically is hourly wage laborers. Usually, the pay for such occupation is lower than that of the white-collar worker, although higher than many entry-level service occupations. Sometimes the work conditions can be strenuous or hazardous and with the rise in skill level that is needed the wages are slowly increasing to the white-collar counterpart level many times higher depending on job requirements. Many industrial Mantainece Mechanics typically drew higher level of wages but are required a higher skill level and the work force to choose from is slowly decreasing in this area not increasing as one might think.

Blue-collar workers exist in varying proportions throughout the industrial world, though some regions are especially noted for their Blue Collar Ethics. The U.S. state of Pennsylvania, particularly the cities of Pittsburgh and Allentown are considered to epitomize the blue-collar ethic. Pittsburgh's blue-collar image is driven largely by media portrayal which is based on the prevailing "hard working blue-collar" mentality that the majority of Pittsburgh residents tend to value. Both cities have sometimes been highlighted in popular culture because of their blue-collar reputations and with the steady loss of these jobs are in financial distress, but according to a 2005 report from the Bureau of Labor Statistics, only 23% of Pittsburgh's job base is made of blue collar occupations. The mid-west lower states have replaced this area with the home of the blue collar worker many industries relocated to the mid-west in the 80's & 90's. With the movement of many Western nations towards service based economy, the number of blue-collar jobs has steadily decreased. Another main reason for the decrease in blue-collar jobs in the United States is due to the technological revolution. Perhaps the biggest reason is that many low-skill manufacturing jobs have been outsourced to developing nations with lower wages. At the same time, some blue-collar workers, predominantly in the building and health care industries, have seen rapidly rising wages due to their requirement of specialized skills.

Chapter Fourteen

There would is a changing place there are many problems that face most industries and how they will survive in the future many times the first thing to go is benefits, Many of us wonder how all that takes place in the big skim of things effects us well it does at many levels to vary different ways we just don't feel it or know it. the average blue collar guy gets up goes to work tries to just make a living to support his family he lives day by day his investment his legacy is his family his kids and the most important thing to him is how his kids will view him. and if he can make time to juggle his job his wife and kids with maybe just a little time for his self this is not in all cases but most the blue collar work probably doesn't have 300,000 or more in the stock exchange doesn't have a great sum of wealth his just a everyday person trying to make it with what he's got you know just like most Americans have sense the beginning of this great country. he or she is the majority not the few wealthy that seem to run things and make calls that effect all of us it's not that we don't wish to be involved with what's going on up above but we spend most day just going about trying to make it. Try to find some solace in this most confusing world.

A good example of how things work for the blue collar worker would be cost of living boy that's some kind of term "cost of living" the biggest bunch of poop ever thought up.

Say a worker makcs 20 dollars an hour works at 40 hours that's 800.00 dollars a week

Now he's going to get a 3 percent raise this year the company is proud of that they are giving 3 percent. Ok that's 60 cents more ok take that times 40 hours that's 24 dollars a week more. Now that's aprox. 100.00 A month more.

Ok his insurance the company provides went up this year 18.00 a week for the family plan now remember he is a family man, so that's 72 dollars a month. And fuel cost per week up from 1.50 to 4.50 a gallon this cost him 75 dollars to fill up instead of 30 dollars once a week by the way a little side not most workers look at fuel cost as how must it takes to make it each week, but I digress back to my go's in to's now that's 45 more dollars a week he needs for fuel. But what it does not there the cost of products used every day went up because of rising fuel. Now his grocery bill went up about 20 dollars a week more. That's 80 dollars a month more

Ok let's add this up 45 plus 80 plus 72 = 197 dollars a month more to just sustain this did not include utilities for the house clothes for the kids you know they are growing and it will take clothes to keep them going. Don't forget school but wait they go to public school that can't cost them! Ok how about school supplies, lunches, the teacher needs funds for things they use in the class room, and no she does not get all that paid by the board or school system. Ok he got a 3 percent cost of living but his live cost way more than this every day he gets up and goes to work. It's not that the blue collar worker is not grateful for what he or she gets but it's not a gift its survival and he or she is slipping backwards every year they reduce benefits while medical cost keep going up. He comes to work sick because he has too, and others get sick this increases more workers coming down with whatever. It's a big circle

and there is no great big answer to this dilemma. I think at times it important not to forget the past while looking in to the future the problems we face now are not that much different from those of the past just more intense do to media hip.

Quotes I will always remember that were past down to me by important people in my life

1. Do UN to others, as you would have them to do UN to you
2. Your word is one of your greatest commodities don't waste it
3. It takes to two make a marriage and two too destroy it
4. Opinions are worth exactly what you pay for it it's free
5. You lead through example
6. If you want full commitment you must give the same

Finally I wish to let all know that I have found no reason to believe that the great values and strong beliefs of the everyday workers are not alive and well.

Author Biography

This is Robert A. Challis's first novel about the working man. He has co-authored other books for previous employers throughout the years. This is important because of Mr. Challis unique insights to having been both a blue collar hourly paid worker and salaried paid management staff member.

Unlike most supervisors and managers he has been a "working supervisor" performing hourly wage tasks and managerial tasks at the same time. This unique perspective allows him insights to how the bridges should be built between management and blue collar workers, as well as a perspective into the thoughts and beliefs of both management and the blue collar workers. His strong team building philosophy has earned him the ability to form group bonding dynamics between both working classes.

His philosophy of "no one man is an island" but a team performs tasks with more efficiency and consistency, than one individual trying to do it alone.